Life is busy ABOVE ground.
What happens BELOW?
Turn the page to peek beneath ...

Beneath the Earth's surface lie layers of soil. Each layer, or horizon, is made of different things. Humus and topsoil are at the top. They have pockets of life and air. Subsoil and loose rock lie further down. They hold rocks, minerals and clay. The deepest horizon is solid rock.

O horizon (humus)

A horizon (topsoil)

WHAT'S BENEATH

# PEEKING
## UNDERGROUND

by Karen Latchana Kenney

illustrated by Steven Wood

Take a look around the park.
What do you see?
People walk and play.
Animals crawl, hop and jump.
Plants stretch towards the sun.

B horizon (subsoil)

C horizon (loose rock)

R horizon (bedrock)

The horizons formed over millions of years. Wind and sun beat
down on the Earth's surface. Water flowed, froze and flowed
again. Rocks, plants and animal remains broke down into smaller
and smaller pieces. The new soil settled into layers.

# Right on top

Humus is the dark, moist top layer of soil. It's made from dead plants and animals. The remains break down into nutrients. Humus is crumbly and light. Air and water pass easily through it.

mushroom

earthworm

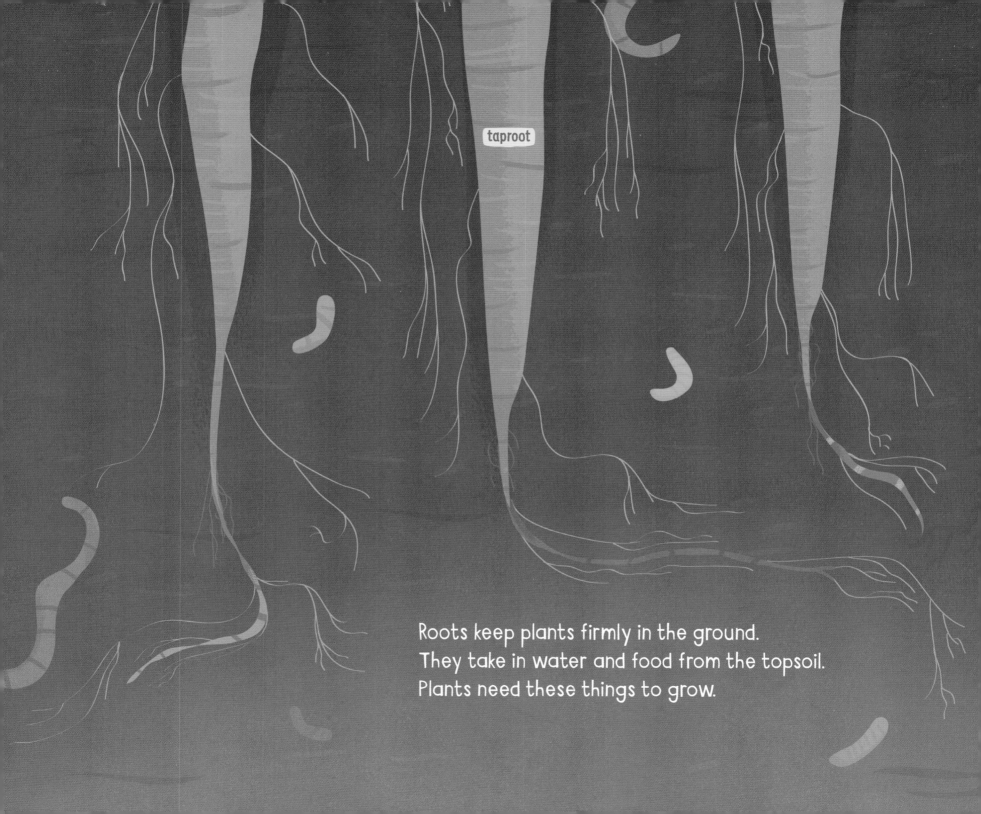

taproot

Roots keep plants firmly in the ground.
They take in water and food from the topsoil.
Plants need these things to grow.

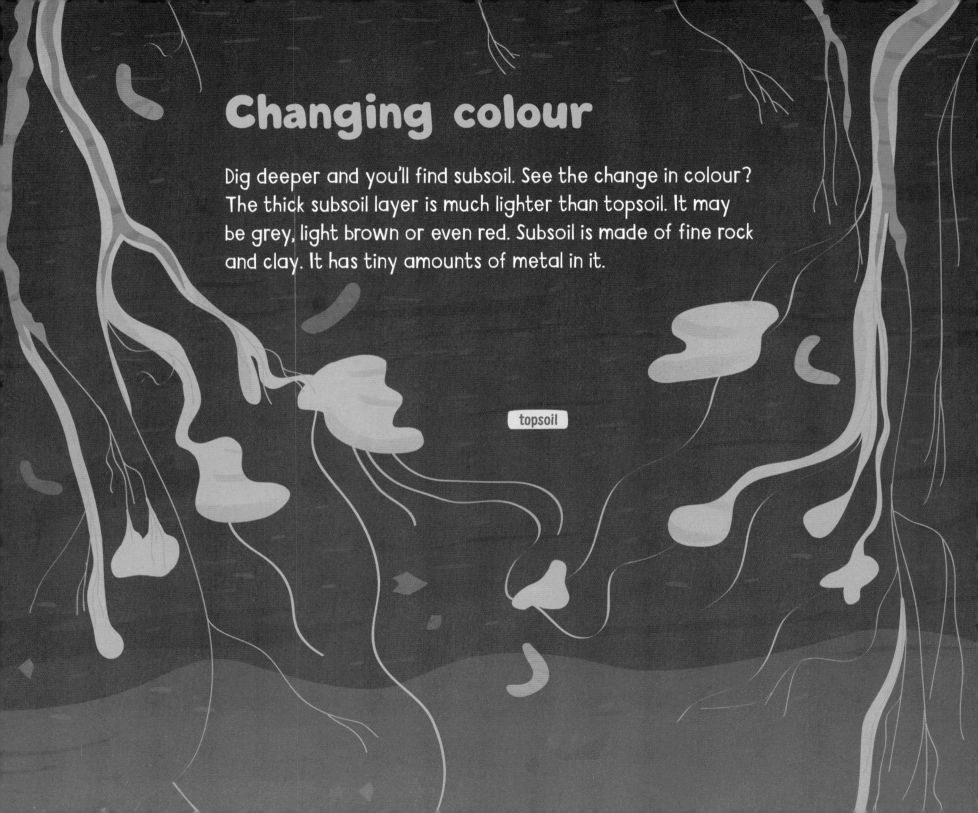

# Changing colour

Dig deeper and you'll find subsoil. See the change in colour? The thick subsoil layer is much lighter than topsoil. It may be grey, light brown or even red. Subsoil is made of fine rock and clay. It has tiny amounts of metal in it.

topsoil

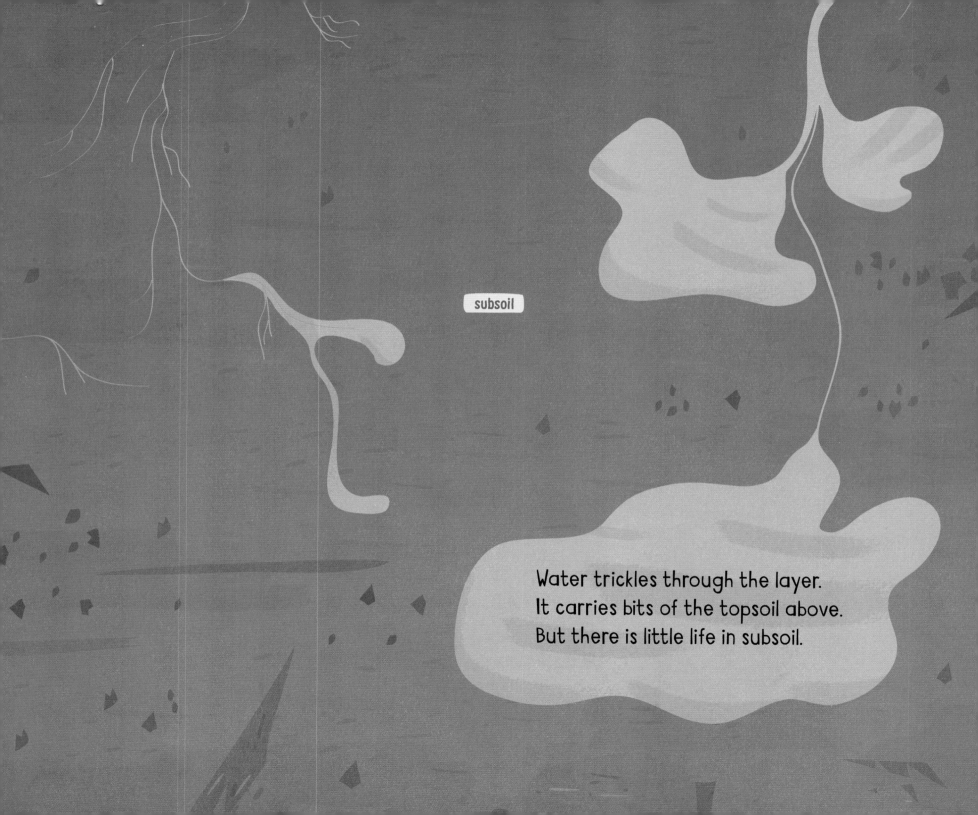

subsoil

Water trickles through the layer.
It carries bits of the topsoil above.
But there is little life in subsoil.

# Follow the water

Water collects above ground in rivers and lakes.
But it also collects underground.

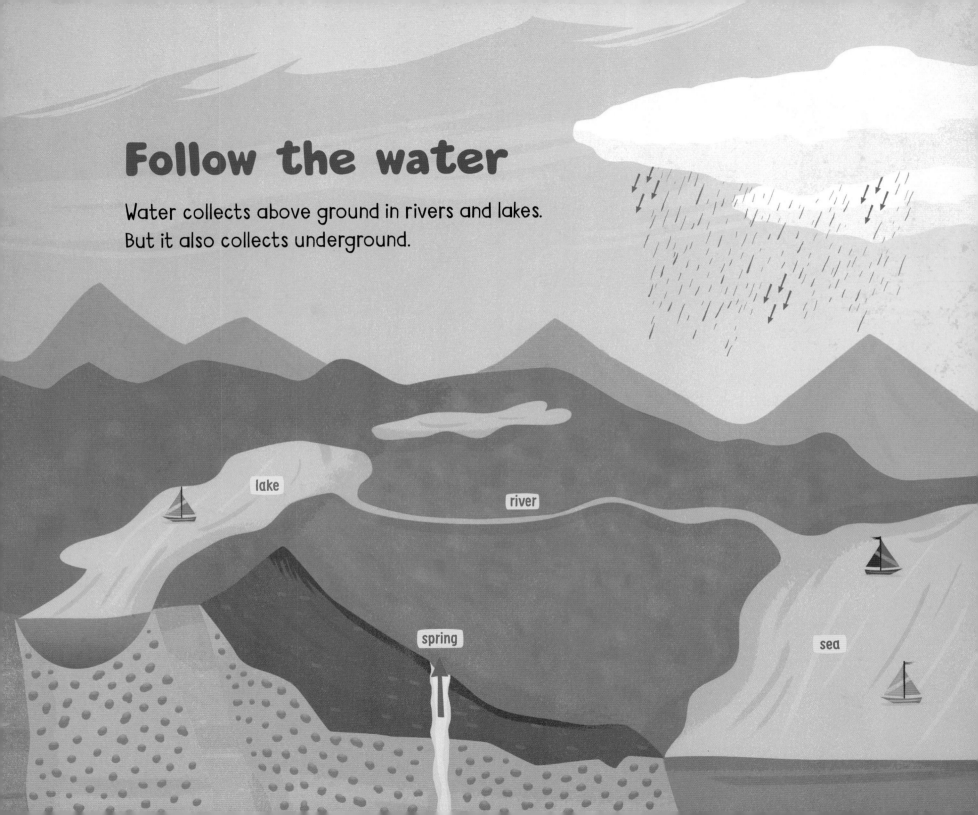

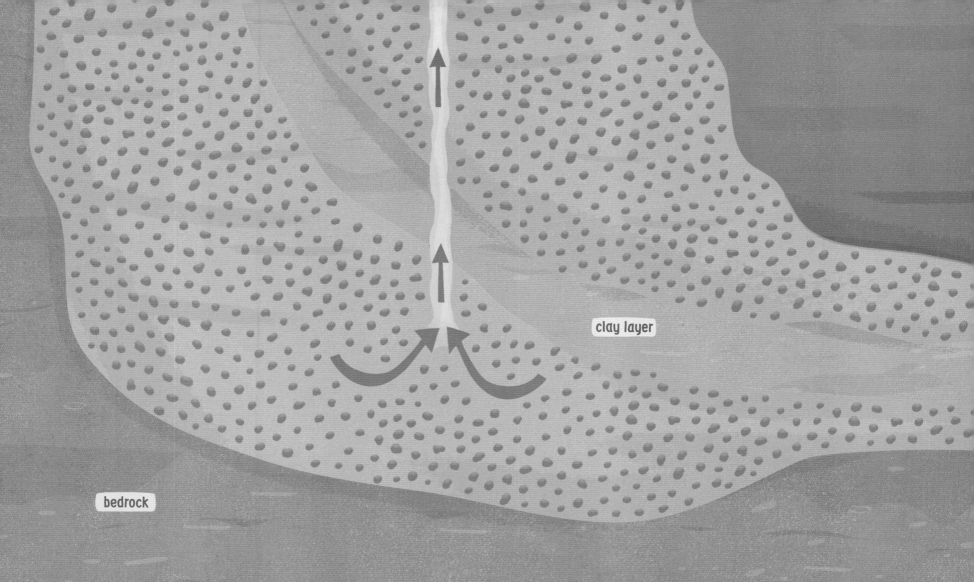

clay layer

bedrock

Water is always moving underground. Rain falls from the sky. It seeps into the soil. Gravity pulls it downwards. Rock takes out much of the bacteria and dirt from the moving water. The water collects in a layer of rock. Some water leaves the rock layer through a spring.

# Simply rock

Rock, rock and more rock! Loose, broken rocks mix with soil just below the subsoil. This layer has minerals such as quartz and mica in it. It rests on top of solid rock. Bedrock is a very deep layer. It sits at the bottom edge of the Earth's crust.

loose rock

bedrock

Bedrock can be many thousands of metres thick. It's often 10 to 100 times thicker than the loose rock layer above it.

# Fossil fuels

Deep inside the bedrock
layer lie fossil fuels.
Oil and natural gas are
fossil fuels. So is coal.

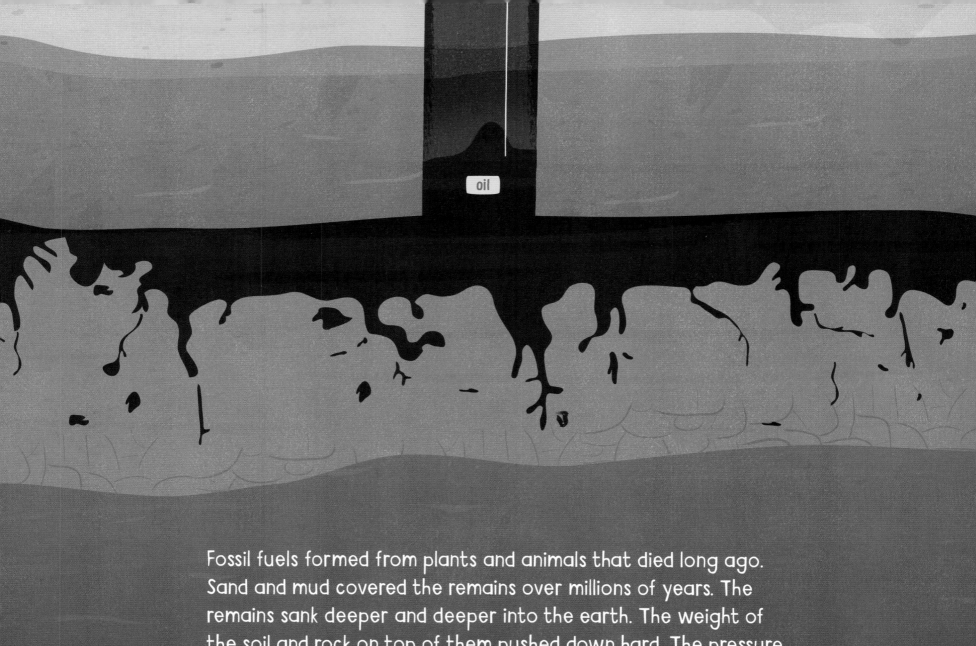

oil

Fossil fuels formed from plants and animals that died long ago.
Sand and mud covered the remains over millions of years. The
remains sank deeper and deeper into the earth. The weight of
the soil and rock on top of them pushed down hard. The pressure
and heat turned the remains into fossil fuels.

# On the move

Earth's crust is not one piece. It is made of seven major plates. See where the two plates below meet? That line is called a fault line.

Ocean crust is heavy. It slides under the land's crust. The two crusts rub together. Sometimes they get stuck. Earthquakes happen when the crusts break free of each other.

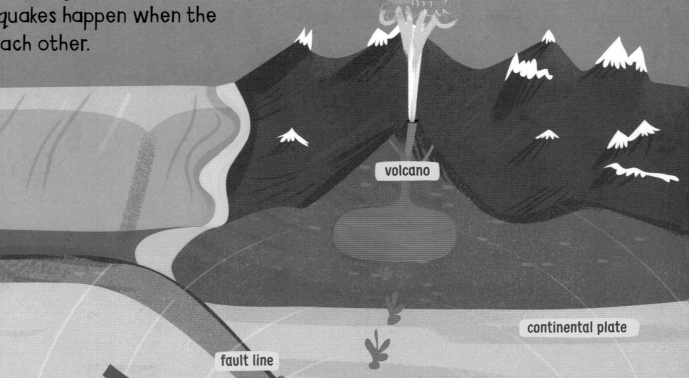

volcano

continental plate

fault line

oceanic plate

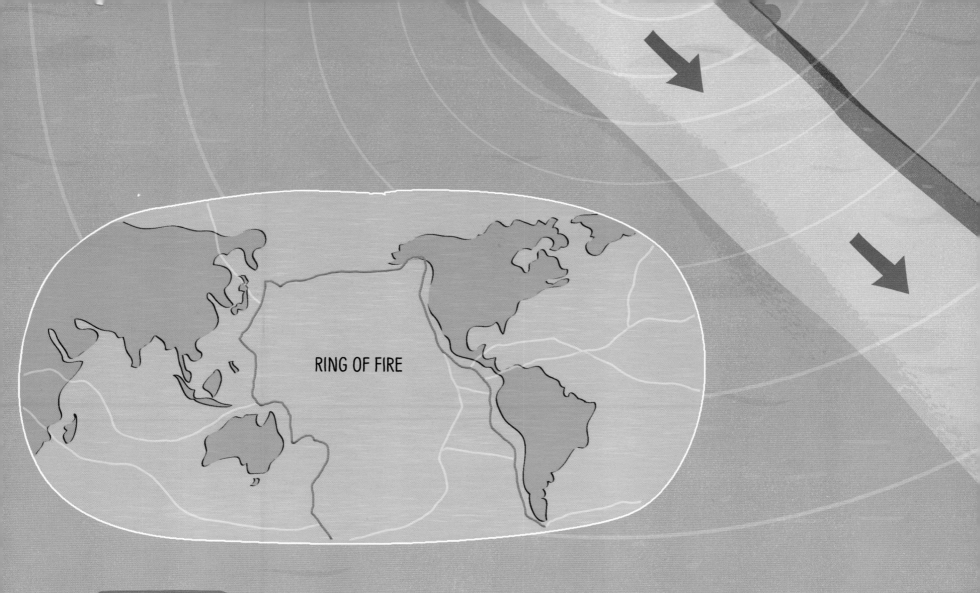

RING OF FIRE

**DID YOU KNOW?**

Many large earthquakes happen in the Ring of Fire. This area stretches along the Pacific Ocean. It's at the edge of the Pacific plate. Many volcanoes also line this plate.

# Volcano blast

What a sight! It's a volcano!

ash

vent

lava

side vent

Take a look inside. See the vent?
It is a crack in the Earth's crust.
Side vents branch off it. Hot, gooey
molten rock called magma is pushed
up the vents. The volcano erupts!
Lava shoots out. Some cools in the
air and becomes ash.

magma

# Below the crust

How far down can we go? The mantle is just below the Earth's crust. It is the Earth's thickest layer. The mantle is 2,900 kilometres (1,800 miles) thick. It is made up of solid and molten rock.

crust

mantle

**DID YOU KNOW?**
People cannot see below the Earth's crust. No machine has gone deep enough to reach the mantle. Scientists make good guesses about what it's like. Much information comes from studying earthquakes. Earthquakes give off waves of energy. These waves tell scientists where and how thick the Earth's layers are.

# To the core

Welcome to the centre of our planet! See the outer core and the inner core? The outer core is mostly liquid metal. It is 2,250 km (1,400 miles) thick. Movement inside the outer core makes the Earth a giant magnet. The Earth's poles are on opposite sides of the magnet.

The inner core looks like a ball. It's the hottest part of our planet. It is 1,200 km (750 miles) thick.

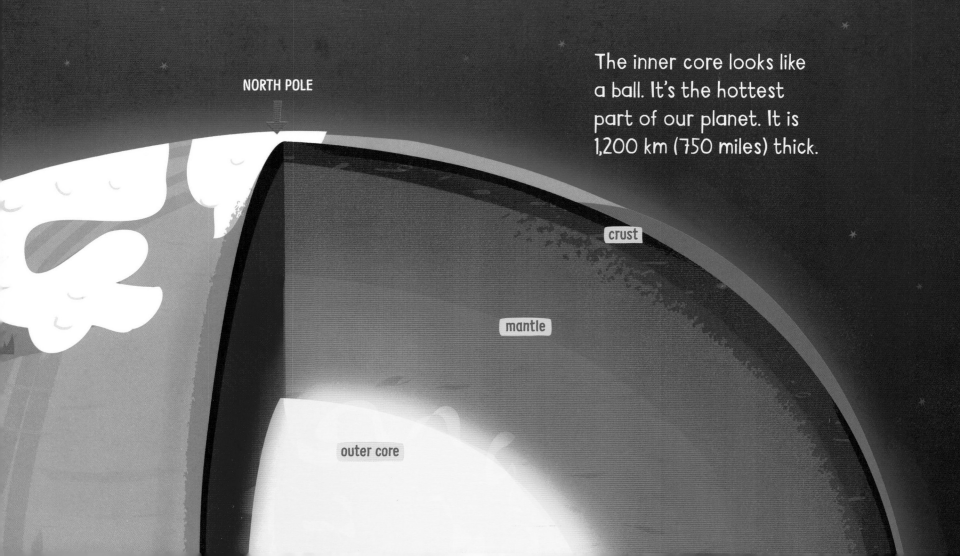

NORTH POLE

crust

mantle

outer core

inner core

SOUTH POLE

Back above ground, bees buzz. Squirrels scurry into the trees. Birds pull earthworms from the soil. The grass tickles your toes. Earth is an amazing place, above the surface or underground!